Freddy
The
Flamingo

Jenny Schreiber
Illustrated by Klarice Southwick

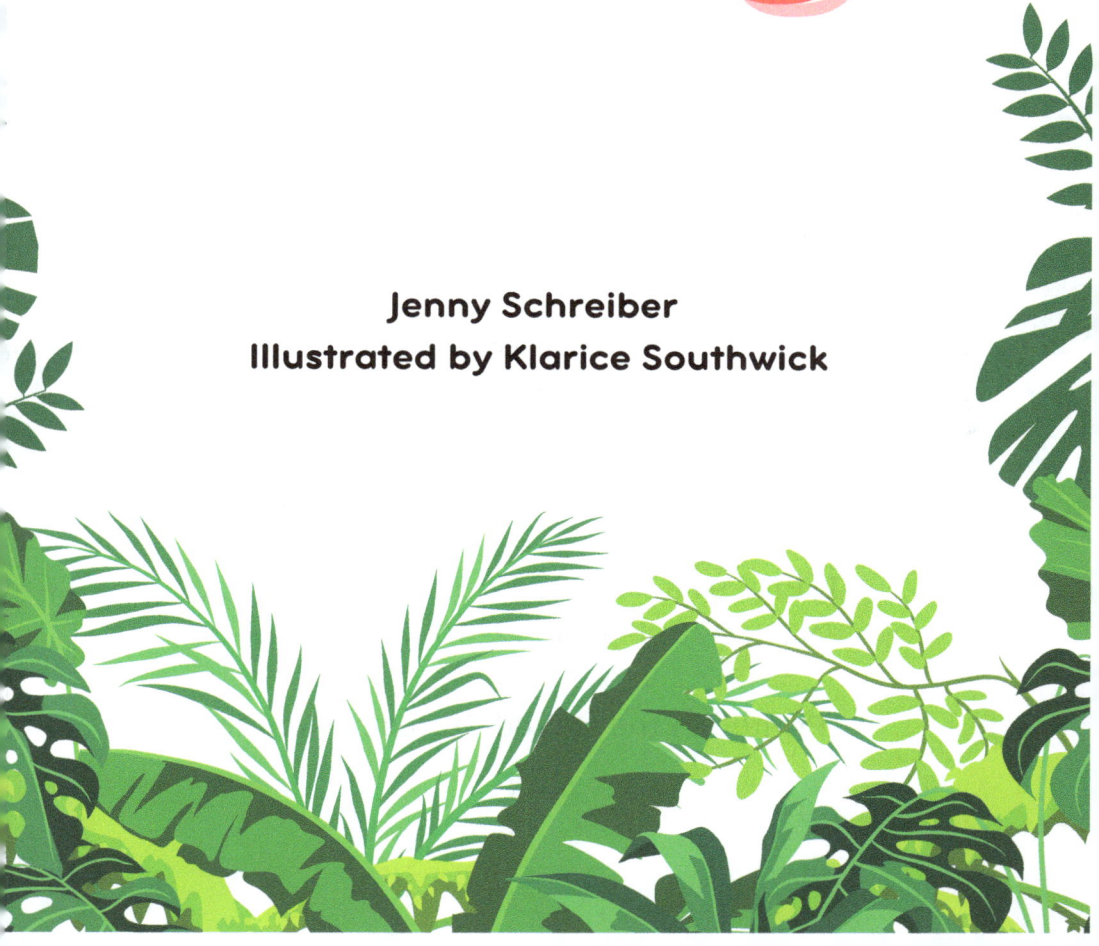

Freddy the Flamingo

Jenny Schreiber
Star Valley, Wy 83110

In Association with:
Elite Online Publishing
63 East 11400 South #230
Sandy, UT 84070
EliteOnlinePublishing.com

Illustrated by Klarice Southwick

ISBN: 978-1-956642-39-1 (Paperback)
ISBN: 978-1-956642-40-7 (Hardcover)

Printed in the United States of America

Freddy The Flamingo

Jenny Schreiber

Illustrated by Klarice Southwick

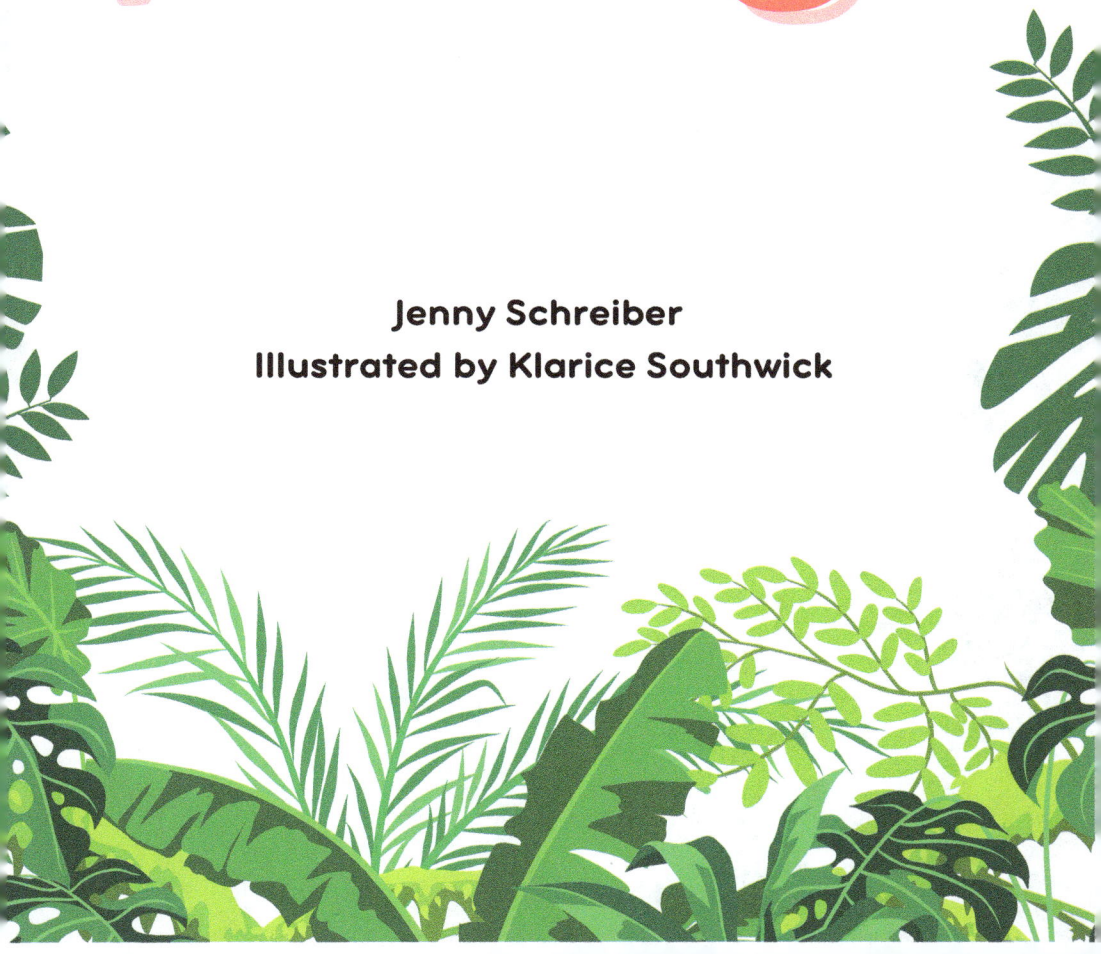

Meet Freddy
the
Flamingo.

Freddy is a wading bird. He loves the water.

His name came from
the Spanish word
Flamengo.
Which means
flame-colored.

He is a crimson/red water nymph.

When Freddy was a
baby chick,
He had white and
grey feathers.
It took him two years
to turn pink/red.

Freddy has long legs. Most of the time he stands on one leg. He can balance many hours on one leg.

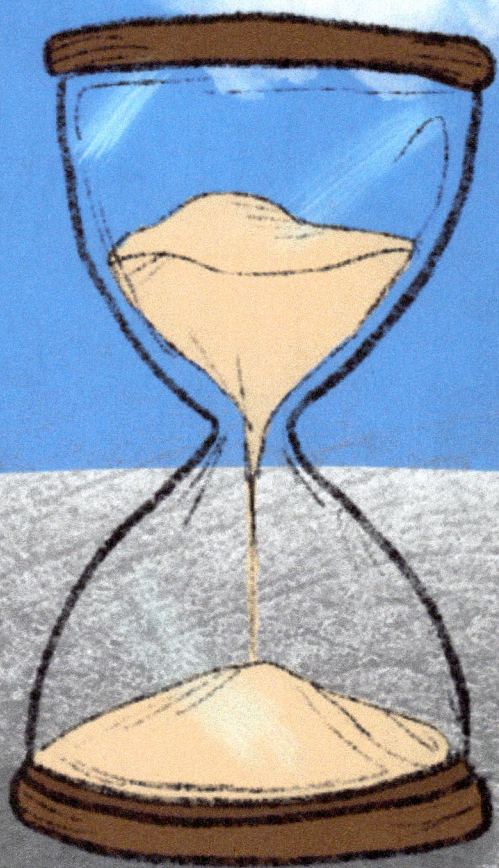

Freddy is a noisy bird.
He sounds like a car.
A little horn honking,
a small grunt, and a
tiny growl.

He is very tall.
As tall as a 6-year-old.
His friends are taller
than him.
Some of them are as
tall as an adult.
4-6 feet.

Freddy weighs
7 pounds (3.18 kg).
The same as a
Pomeranian dog.

His wings spread
up to
37 inches.
About as big
as a bike.

Freddy flies high in the sky with his friends. He migrates to find more food.

He eats brine shrimp
and blue-green algae
as well as insect larvae,
small insects, mollusks,
and crustaceans.

Freddy can eat thousands of tiny shrimp per day! The more he eats, the more pink/red he gets.

Freddy can eat thousands of tiny shrimp per day! The more he eats, the more pink/red he gets.

Freddy is a social bird and hangs with thousands of his friends.

When Freddy hangs with his family, of 50 or more flamingos, it is called Flamboyance.

Flamboyance

If a predator comes near, he and his friends start running in a zig-zag pattern. It is a fast escape.

Freddy can live
a long life,
up to 83 years old.

Freddy is closely related
to the Penguin.
They are both
water birds.

Freddy is an American flamingo. He lives in southern Florida. He has cousins that live in Europe, Asia, and Africa.

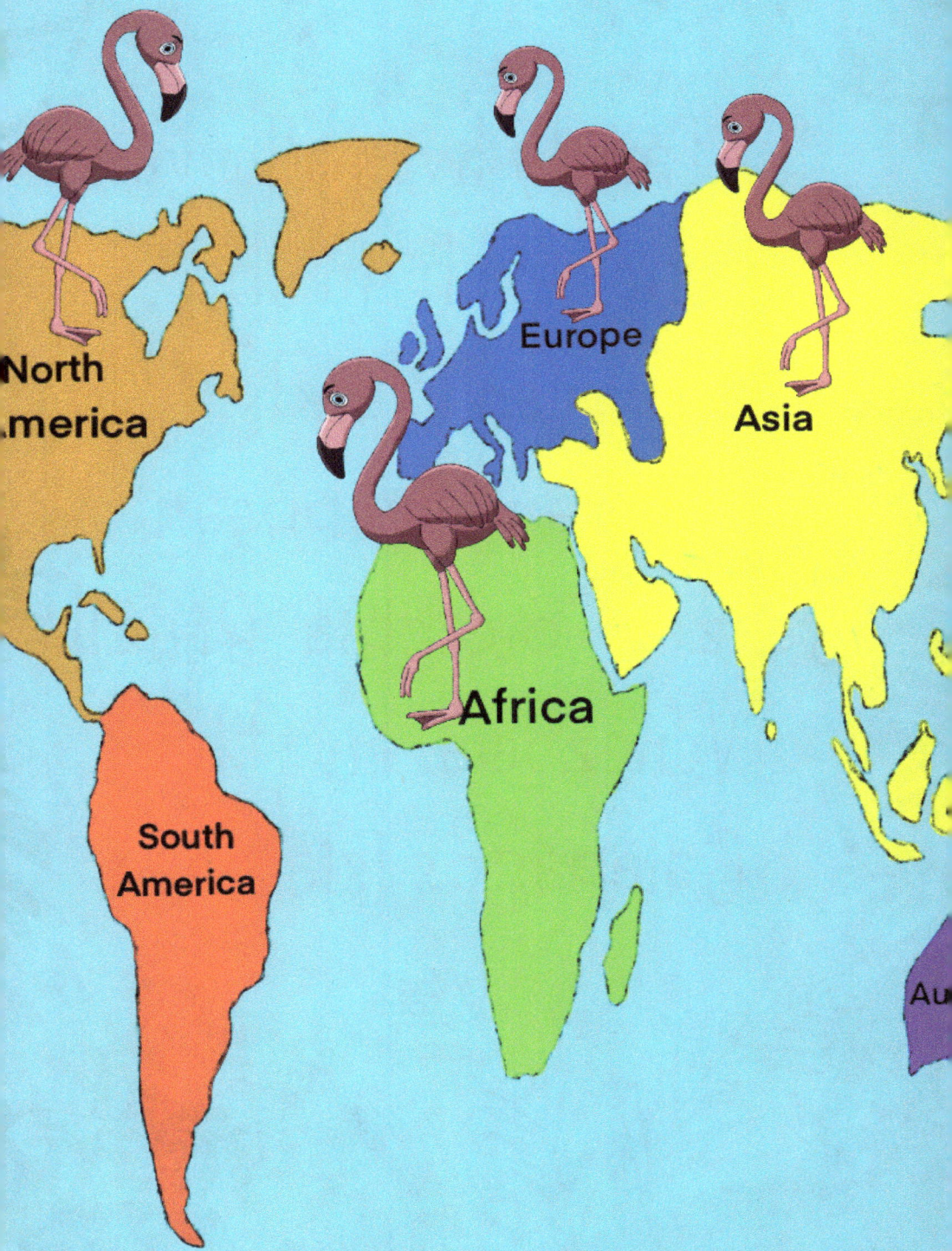

North
America

Europe

Asia

Africa

South
America

Au

His family lives all over the earth. In the Caribbean islands, the Mexican Caribbean, Belize, Colombia, Brazil, Venezuela, and the Galápagos Islands.

THE END

www.ingramcontent.com/pod-product-compliance
Lightning Source LLC
Chambersburg PA
CBHW071823050426

42335CB00063BA/1780